What do you call a fat Chinaman?
    A chunk.

How many gays does it take to change a light bulb?
    Seven. One to change the bulb, and six to shriek, "Faaaaabulous!"

What's the difference between garbage and a girl from New Jersey?
    Sometimes garbage gets picked up.

How did Helen Keller burn her ear?
    Answering the iron.

What can you do with a dog with no legs?
    Take it for a drag.

Did you hear about the man who was half Polish and half Italian?
    He made himself an offer he couldn't understand.

. . . Look inside for even more

Truly Tasteless Jokes

Truly Tasteless Jokes

✻ Blanche Knott ✻

BALLANTINE BOOKS · NEW YORK

Copyright © 1982 by Blanche Knott

All rights reserved under International and Pan-American Copyright Conventions. Published in the United States by Ballantine
Books, a division of Random House, Inc., New York, and si-
multaneously in Canada by Random House of Canada Limited.
Toronto.

Library of Congress Catalog Card Number: 81-22883

ISBN 0-345-32920-1

Manufactured in the United States of America

First Edition: August 1982
Fifty-eighth Printing: May 1989

To my mother

I am indebted to countless people for their contributions, but all refused to have their names associated in any way with this book.

Contents

Truly
Tasteless
Jokes

Dead Baby

What does it take to make a dead baby float?
One scoop of ice cream and a scoop of dead
baby.

How did the dead baby cross the road?
Stapled to the chicken.

What's the difference between unloading a truckload of dead babies and a truckload of bowling
balls?
You can use a pitchfork on the dead babies.

Why do they boil water when a baby's being born?
So that if it's born dead, they can make soup.

How do you fit a thousand dead babies in a phone booth?
La Machine!

How do you get them out?
With a straw!

What's red and squirms in the corner?
A baby playing with a razor blade.

What's blue and squirms in the corner?
A baby in a baggie.

What's green and sits in the corner?
The same baby two weeks later.

What's red and hangs from the ceiling?
A baby on a meathook.

Why do you put a baby in the blender feet first?
So you can watch its expression.

What's the perfect gift for a dead baby?
 A dead puppy.

What's red and goes around and around?
 A baby in a garbage disposal.

What's red and bubbly and scratches at the window?
 A baby in a microwave.

Helen Keller

How did Helen Keller burn her fingers?
Reading the waffle iron.

How did Helen Keller's mother punish her?
By rearranging the living-room furniture.

How did Helen Keller meet her husband?
It was a blind date.

Why were Helen Keller's fingers purple?
She heard it through the grapevine.

What did Helen Keller do when she fell down the well?
She screamed her hands off.

Did you hear about the Helen Keller doll?
　　Wind it up and it walks into walls.

*

Why does Helen Keller masturbate with one hand?
　　So she can moan with the other.

*

Why did Helen Keller's dog jump off a cliff?
　　You would too if your name was
　　Uggggrrrgggh.

*

Why was Helen Keller's leg yellow?
　　Her dog was blind, too.

*

How did Helen Keller go crazy?
　　Trying to read a stucco wall.

*

How did Helen Keller burn her ear?
　　Answering the iron.

*

What did Helen Keller's parents do to punish her for swearing?
　　Washed her hands with soap.

Did you hear about Helen Keller's new book?
   Around the Block in Eighty Days

How does Helen Keller drive?
   With one hand on the wheel and one hand on
   the road.

What's Helen Keller's favorite color?
   Corduroy.

Polish

Did you hear that the Polish government bought a thousand septic tanks?

As soon as they learn to drive them, they're going to invade Russia.

Did you hear about the new Polish drink?

Perrier and club soda.

Why does the Pole always take a dime along on his dates?

So that if he can't come, he can call.

Why were the Poles pushing their house down the road in the middle of the winter?

They were trying to jump-start the furnace.

A Pole suspected his wife of infidelity and began to follow her movements. Sure enough, his suspicions were justified. Coming home from work early, he burst into the bedroom, catching his wife and lover in the act, and, crazed with grief, he put the pistol to his own head.

"Don't laugh!" he shouted when his wife burst out in giggles. "You're next!"

*

"Knock, knock."
   "Who's there?"
   "Polish burglar."

*

A group of scientists discovered an apelike creature in the wilds which they were certain was the Missing Link. The proof of their theory, though, required that a human mate with the ape in order to see what characteristics the progeny would take on. So they put an ad in the paper: "$5000 to Mate with Ape."

The next morning a Pole called up in response to the ad and said he'd be willing to be part of the experiment. "But," he said, "I have three conditions."

The scientists agreed to hear him out.

"First: My wife must never know.

"Second: The children must be raised as Catholics.

"Third: If I can pay in installments, I'm definitely interested."

Ever seen the Polish sex manual?

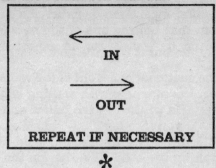

Why did the Pole spend all night outside the whorehouse?

>He was waiting for the red light to turn green.

Lick cover of a book of matches, then bend it back so matches are exposed. Stick to forehead.
Ask, "What am I?"

>A Polish miner.

Did you hear about the Polish starlet?

>She went to Hollywood and fucked the writer.

The manager of a prosperous whorehouse in Warsaw one night found, to his dismay, that he was short of girls for the evening's entertainment. Thinking quickly, he dashed out and bought several inflatable fuck dolls, figuring that, given his average clientele, no one would know the difference. Soon he ushered a customer into a room that housed one of the new lovelies, assuring him he was in for an especially good time.

When the customer came out of the room a little while later, the manager was waiting eagerly in the hallway. He winked at the fellow and asked, "Well? How'd you like her?"

"I don't know what happened," said the customer, shaking his head. "I bit her on the tit, she farted, and flew out the window."

A stranger walks into a bar and announces to the barman, "Hey, fella! Have I got some terrific Polish jokes for you guys."

The bartender leans over to him and says, "Listen, if I were you I'd watch your tongue. The two 250-pound bouncers are Polish, I'm Polish and I ain't no midget, and every man in here is Polish."

"Oh, that's okay," said the stranger cheerfully. "I'll talk v-e-r-y s-l-o-w-l-y."

Do you know why the suicide rate in Poland is so low?

Because you can't jump out of a basement window.

How can you tell a Polish Peeping Tom?
    (Pull out front of own pants and look down.)

Why do Polish people have such beautiful noses?
    They're handpicked.

Did you hear about the two Polish hunters?
    They were driving along when they came up
    to a sign that said "Bear Left," so they went
    home.

Or the Polish hunters who got themselves all set up for a weekend of hunting? They gathered their guns and the dogs and the ammunition and the orange hats and tromped about for hours, but with no luck whatsoever. And when they came out of the woods at dusk, they looked around at all the other hunters, who were carrying braces of pheasant and quail, ducks and geese, even a deer or two.

"Gee," said one Pole to his companion, "everyone else seems to be doing pretty well for themselves. Whaddaya think we could be doing wrong?"

"I dunno," said the other. "Maybe we're not throwing the dogs high enough."

What do you call a pretty girl in Poland?
A tourist.

Two Polish guys went away on their annual hunting expedition, and by accident one was shot by the other. His worried companion got him out of the deep woods, into the car, and off to the nearest hospital.

"Well, Doc," he inquired anxiously, "is he going to make it?"

"It's tough," said the doctor. "He'd have a better chance if you hadn't gutted him first."

A realtor is showing a new property to an affluent young couple, who are somewhat bewildered by his behavior. On every landing, the realtor stops to open the window and shout, "Green side up!" Finally, they ask why.

"I've got a Pole laying the sod," he explains, "and I've got to make sure he does it right."

Did you hear about the guy who made a million dollars in Poland with Cheerios?
He sold them as doughnut seeds.

Did you hear about the Polish car pool?
They all meet at work.

How come Poles don't go elephant hunting?
They get too tired carrying the decoys.

How come Poles don't become pharmacists?
They can't fit the little bottles in the typewriter.

How do you know when your house has been burgled by a Pole?
The garbage's been eaten and the dog is pregnant.

Did you hear about the Polish bank?
You bring in a toaster and they give you ten thousand dollars.

A young Polish girl was hitchhiking along the Interstate, and a big semi pulled over to pick her up. The driver was a serious CB addict, and the dashboard boasted an enormous CB radio.

"That's the best radio ever made," he explained to the bug-eyed girl. "You can talk anywhere in the *world* with it."

"No kidding," she gasped. "Boy, I would really love to talk to my mother in Poland."

"Oh, yeah?"

"I would give anything to talk to my mother in Poland."

"*Anything?*" he asked.

"Anything," she assured him.

"Well, maybe we can work something out," he leered, pulling his cock, by this time erect, out of his pants.

So the girl leaned over, bent down, and said loudly, "HELLO, MOM?"

*

What are the three most difficult years for a Pole?
  Second grade.

*

Did you hear about the Pole who had a penis transplant?
  His hand rejected it.

*

Two Poles are out fishing for the day, and they have a hell of a time: fish grabbing the hooks as fast as they can get them into the water. Finally, with the boat as full of fish as possible, they decide it's time to head for shore.

"But listen," says Stan, "why don't we mark the spot?"

"No problem," says Jerzy, who dives in and paints a big black X on the bottom of the boat.

Stan beams with pleasure, and they're almost back to the dock when his face wrinkles in consternation. "Oh, no!" he cries to Jerzy, "what if we don't get the same boat?"

What's this?

A Polish coke spoon.

What does a Polish girl do after she sucks cock?
Spits out the feathers.

What do Poles wear to weddings?
Formal bowling shirts.

Did you hear about the Pole who locked his family
in the car?
He had to get a coathanger to get them out.

A Pole walks into his local bar and goes straight up to the bartender, who turns away in disgust at the handful of horseshit the Pole is holding.

"Hey, Harry," says the Pole, "look what I almost stepped in."

A young Polish guy wanted more than anything to become a cop, and went through the rigorous entrance exam, the last question of which was "Who killed Christ?" The would-be rookie went home excitedly and said to his wife, "Honey, I think they're putting me on a murder case!"

Jewish

What's the Jewish version of foreplay?
Half an hour of begging.

Do you know how to keep Jews out of the country club?
Let one in, and he'll keep the rest out.

This black guy was walking down 125th Street, kicking rubbish out of his way, when he spotted something amid the trash that gleamed strangely. It turned out to be an oddly shaped bottle, and when he rubbed it, a Jewish genie appeared. "I'll give you two wishes," intoned the genie.

"Far out," said the black guy. "First, I want to be white, uptight, and out of sight. Second, I want to be surrounded by warm, sweet pussy."

So the genie turned him into a tampon.

The moral of the story: You can't get anything from a Jew without strings attached.

Why is money green?
    Because the Jews pick it before it's ripe.

Why did the Jews wander in the desert for forty years?
    Somebody dropped a quarter.

Why do Jews have such big noses?
    Because air is free.

What happens when a Jew with an erection walks into a wall?
    He breaks his nose.

What's a Jewish dilemma?
    Free ham.

What's the definition of a queer Jew?
    Someone who likes girls more than money.

How do you stop a Jewish girl from fucking you?
    Marry her.

Did you hear about the bum who walked up to the Jewish mother on the street and said, "Lady, I haven't eaten in three days."

"Force yourself," she replied.

*

Why do JAPs use gold diaphragms?

Their husbands like coming into money.

*

What's the difference between karate and judo?

Karate is a method of self-defense, and judo is what bagels are made of.

*

What's the difference between a JAP and poverty?

Poverty sucks.

*

How did they know Jesus was Jewish?

Because he lived at home until he was thirty, he went into his father's business, his mother thought he was God—and he thought his mother was a virgin.

*

How do you tickle a JAP?

Gucci, Gucci, goo.

How many JAPs does it take to change a light bulb?

Two. One to call Daddy, and one to get out the Diet Pepsi.

*

What do JAPs make for dinner?

Reservations.

How does a JAP eat a banana? (This is a visual joke, so pay attention.)

Pretend you are holding a banana in your right hand. With left hand, peel off the three or four strips of peel about halfway down the banana. Continuing to hold peeled banana in right hand, place left hand behind head. Force head down over banana.

Why do JAPs wear bikinis?

To separate the meat from the fish.

*

What do you get when you cross a JAP and a hooker?

Someone who sucks credit cards.

How many Jewish mothers does it take to change a light bulb?

"None, dahling, I'll sit in the dark . . ."

Did you hear that the limbo was invented by the Jews?

Yeah, from sneaking into pay toilets.

A Palestinian gentleman was taking a walk on the West Bank when he was brutally beaten by a gang of young Israeli toughs. Deciding to take matters into his own hands, he bought a huge German Shepherd trained to kill on command and went out to seek revenge.

It didn't take him long to see the perfect victim: a little old Jewish man walking a little dog that somewhat resembled a dachshund. The Palestinian loosed his ferocious dog—but to his astonishment he saw the little dog pin his dog to the ground and swallow his dog whole, all within thirty seconds.

"What kind of dog *is* that?" he gasped, ashen-faced.

"Well, before we had his nose fixed he used to be an alligator," explained the little Jewish man.

WASP

What's the definition of a WASP?
Someone who gets out of the shower to pee.

How many WASPs does it take to change a light bulb?
Two. One to mix the martinis, and one to call the electrician.

What do WASPs say after they make love?
"Thank you very much; it'll never happen again."

How can you tell the bride at a WASP wedding?
She's the one kissing the golden retriever.

Where do WASPs eat?
Restaurants.

What do you call a WASP who doesn't work for his father, isn't a lawyer, and believes in social causes?

A failure.

*

How can you tell the only WASP in a sauna?

He's the one with the *Wall Street Journal* on his lap.

*

What's a WASP's idea of a welfare check?

An Irish tartan.

*

Why did God create WASPs?

Somebody had to buy retail.

*

How do WASPs wean their young?

By firing the maid.

*

What's a WASP's idea of open-mindedness?

Dating a Canadian.

*

What do you get when you cross a Jew and a WASP?

A pushy Pilgrim.

What do you get when you cross a WASP and an orangutan?

>I don't know, but whatever it is, it won't let you in *its* cage.

What do you get when you cross a WASP and a Puerto Rican?

>Assault and battery.

How can you tell a male WASP is sexually excited?

>By the stiff upper lip.

How many WASPs does it take to plan a trip to Israel?

>Two. One to ask where, and one to ask why.

What do little girl WASPs want to be when they grow up?

>"The very best person I possibly can."

Why did the WASP cross the road?

>To get to the middle.

What's a WASP's idea of foreplay?
    Drying the dishes.

How can you tell the WASPs in a Chinese restaurant?
    They're the ones not sharing the food.

What's a WASP's idea of post-coital depression?
    Not being able to reach *The New Yorker* from
    bed.

How does a WASP propose marriage?
    He asks, "How would you like to be buried
    with my people?"

    Two WASPs were making love when the man
looked down and said, "Did I hurt you?"
    "No," she replied. "Why?"
    "You moved."

Black

This black guy walks into a bar with a beautiful parrot on his shoulder.

"Wow!" says the bartender. "That is really something. Where'd you get it?"

"Africa," says the parrot.

What has six legs and goes "Ho-de-do, ho-de-do, ho-de-do?"

Three blacks running for the elevator.

What's another word for cocoon?

N-nigger.

What's black and white and goes rolling along the boardwalk?

A black and a pigeon fighting over a chicken wing.

How do you shoot a black man?
    Aim for the radio.

What do you call a black boy with a bicycle?
    Thief!

What's the new Webster's definition of the word
"confusion?"
    Father's Day in Harlem.

What's the new Webster's definition of the word
"reneg?"
    Shift change at the carwash.

A black guy knew he had it made when the old
brass bottle he found in the back yard turned out
to have a genie in it. Any three wishes he had
would be granted, the genie informed him.
    "I wanna be rich," said the black man. The back
yard filled up with chests of gold coins and jewels
in the blinking of an eye.
    "I'm no fool," said the black. "I wanna be white."
And there he stood, white, blond-haired and blue-
eyed.
    "Thirdly, I never want to work another day in
my life."
    And he was black again.

A successful black banker got into the latest fad: hang gliding. He went out and bought a beautiful, sky-blue jumpsuit, took his hang glider, and proceeded to float off over the woods.

Two old white farmers, Royce and J.T., had picked the same day to do a little hunting. Royce looked up and said to J.T., "Shit! Dat's de biggest goddam bird I eva seen!"

"Let's get em," said J.T.

They fired off several rounds, but the glider floated serenely over the trees and out of sight.

"Hell, Royce," said J.T., "I b'lieve we dusted dat bird."

"Shit, I *know* we dusted em," said Royce. "Did you see how fast it dropped dat nigger?"

What do you get when you bury a thousand blacks up to their necks?

Afroturf.

An old Southern planter goes into the hospital and is informed by the doctor that his condition is pretty serious. In fact, he's going to require a heart transplant.

"Well, doctor," drawls the planter, "you'd best get on with it. But whatever you do, just don't give me the heart of a nigger."

When he comes out of the anesthetic, the doctor is leaning over his bedside anxiously. "Cal," he says, "I got some good news and some bad news. I *had* to use a nigger's heart."

Cal pales.

"But the good news is: Your dick is three inches longer.

What do you call a black millionaire industrialist?
    A tycoon.

What do you call a black Frenchman?
    Jacques Custodian.

What do you call a black test-tube baby?
    Janitor in a Drum.

Do you know why so many blacks were killed in Vietnam?
    Because every time the sergeant said "Get down," they stood up and started dancing.

Why are the palms of black people's hands white?
    Because they were all leaned up against cop cars when God spray-painted.

Did you hear about the new perfume for black women?
    It's called Eau-de-doo-dah-day.

How do you keep little black kids from jumping up and down on the bed?
    Put Velcro on the ceiling.

What color's a black who's run over by a steamroller?
    Flat black.

Ethnic Jokes – Variegated

Why didn't the black man want to marry a Mexican?
  He didn't want the kids to grow up too lazy to steal.

Do you know about the world's shortest books?
  Polish Wit and Wisdom
  Jewish Business Ethics
  Italian War Heroes
  and *Negroes I Have Met While Yachting*

How can you tell there's an Irishman present at a cockfight?
  He enters a duck.
How can you tell a Pole is present?
  He bets on the duck.
How can you tell an Italian is present?
  The duck wins.

Do you know the Irish definition of foreplay?

"Brace yourself, Bridget!"

"Help! Help!" cried the young woman as she staggered up the steps of the police station. "An Irishman molested me!"

"How'd you know he was Irish?" inquired the sergeant at the desk.

"I had to help him," she gasped.

"Dad," said the kid, "can I have five dollars to buy a guinea pig?"

"Here's ten dollars, son. Go find yourself a nice Irish girl."

Did you hear about the man who was half Polish and half Italian?

He made himself an offer he couldn't understand.

A Jew, a Hindu, and an Irishman were traveling together, and as night fell they came to a little country inn. The innkeeper explained apologetically that only two beds were available in the inn but that he would be glad to make up a comfortable cot for the third man in the barn. So the three travelers drew straws, and it fell upon the Jew to sleep in the barn.

In a few minutes there was a knock on the door, to which the innkeeper responded. "I'm so sorry," explained the Jew, "but there is a pig in the barn, and my religion forbids me to sleep under the same roof as a pig."

The Hindu had taken the next straw, and out he went. In a few minutes, though, there was another knock, and the innkeeper opened the door on the Indian fellow. Apologizing gracefully, he explained that his religious persuasion forbade him to share shelter with a cow, and there was indeed such a creature in the barn.

Finally, out went the Irishman. In a few minutes there was yet another knock on the door, which the innkeeper answered. On the sill stood the pig and the cow.

An Italian, a Pole, and a black man moved out to California to seek their fortunes. The Italian and the black got jobs right away, but weeks went by without the Pole finding employment. Finally, one evening he announced to his roommates that he had a big interview the next morning at nine and, setting the alarm well ahead of time, he went to bed.

In the middle of the night the other two snuck into his room, smeared his face and hands with blackface, and set the alarm forward. When it went off in the morning, the Pole leaped from his bed, pulled on his clothes, and dashed off so as not to be late for the critical interview.

The interviewer invited him in with an apologetic expression on his face. "I'm sorry to have brought you here for nothing," he said, "but I'm afraid we simply don't employ blacks."

"Blacks! What are you talking about?" sputtered the Pole. "My name is Joe Bukarski!"

"I'm so sorry, Mister Bukarski, but we simply don't make any exceptions in our hiring policy."

"But I'm not black!"

"I'm sorry you're taking it so hard. You may not think you're black, but have you looked in a mirror lately?"

The Pole got up and went over to a mirror near the door. Staring in disbelief at his undeniably black reflection, he stammered, "Oh my God—they woke the wrong guy!"

The Italian and the Polish parachutists were arguing about who was best at folding a parachute. Unable to resolve their dispute on the ground, they decided to go up in the plane and judge by the mid-air performance of their chutes. The Pole jumped first, pulled the cord, and started floating toward the earth. The Italian jumped, pulled the cord—and nothing happened. He pulled the safety cord—nothing. In a matter of seconds he whizzed past the Pole, plummeting like a stone.

"Oh," shouted the Pole, yanking off his harness, "so ya wanna race!"

A Jew and a Chinaman were in a bar together. The Jew brought up the subject of Pearl Harbor, reprimanding the Chinaman for the disgraceful

38

role his countrymen had played. He protested vehemently, pointing out that the raid had been made by the Japanese, and that China was in no way to blame.

"Japanese, Chinese, they're all the same to me," retorted the Jew.

Pretty soon the Chinese fellow started talking about the tragic sinking of the *Titanic*, asking the guy if he didn't feel some degree of personal responsibility about it.

"Hey, wait a minute!" protested the guy. "The Jews didn't have anything to do with the sinking of the *Titanic*—it was sunk by an iceberg!"

"Iceberg, Goldberg," said the Chinaman, "they're all the same to me."

What's eight miles long and has an IQ of forty?
The St. Patrick's Day Parade.

A widower was devoted to his only daughter and naturally was concerned when she decided not only to get married but to marry a Greek. Blushing furiously, he sat her down to discuss the facts of life, but she brushed him off, assuring him she knew all about those things and not to worry.

"Well, just one thing," the father implored. "If he asks you to turn over, you don't have to."

The young couple got married and were extremely happy until about six months had gone by. Embracing his wife in bed, the Greek said, "Why don't you roll over, dearest?"

"Oh, no, you don't!" she said. "My father said if I don't want to, I don't have to."

"Whatsamatter," he said, "don't you wanna get pregnant?"

Sammy Davis, Jr. stepped onto a bus in Jacksonville, and the bus driver said, "Nigger, get to the back of the bus."

"But I'm Jewish," protested Davis.

"Get off."

An Italian, a Jew, and a Greek were walking down the sidewalk when—ZAP—a bolt of lightning came down and killed all three instantly. Up they went to the gates of heaven, where St. Peter greeted them warmly.

"Saint Peter, you can't do this to us," they protested vehemently. "We're young men in the prime of life. *Please* let us go on living."

St. Peter pondered the issue. "Well," he finally pronounced, "I'll let you go back to Earth on one condition: that from this moment on, you all promise to abstain from your one most favorite activity."

The young men lost no time in giving their fervent promises, and—WHAM—found themselves back walking down the sidewalk. What should they come across on the corner but a pizza parlor. The Italian broke into a sweat. Unable to resist temptation, he dashed in, ordered a slice, took a bite, and—POOF!—vanished in a puff of smoke. The Jew and Greek were understandably sobered by this event and continued walking, when a quarter rolled across the sidewalk.

His eyes lighting up, the Jew bent over to pick it up.

And the Greek disappeared.

What do you call a fat Chinaman?
    A chunk.

What do you get when you cross a Mexican and an Iranian?
    Oil of Olé.

Did you hear about the football game between Italy and Poland? The Italians all started arguing about who was going to be quarterback and walked off the field, and three plays later the Poles won.

A Pole, an Italian, and an Irishman have planned an expedition across the Sahara, and at the appointed time each shows up with the baggage critical to his survival.

Motioning to his flask, the Irishman says, "It's going to be a thirsty business, this crossing the desert, and I'll need a drop to drink."

Nodding his approval, the Italian points out his

potful of pasta. "Itsa gonna be hungry work," he says.

They look across at the Pole, who is carrying nothing but a turquoise-and-white left front door to a '57 Chevy. "It's going to be plenty hot out there," he explains, "and I want to be able to roll down the window."

✳

A Pole, an Italian and a Jew are marooned on an island. While walking along the beach, one of them comes across an old bottle. He rubs it and out comes a genie, who is empowered to grant them each their dearest wish.

"Ah," says the Italian, "let me go back to the Old Country, where the wine is sweet and the women are beautiful." Poof!—he vanishes.

"For me," says the Jew, "I want to go to the Holy Land and live out the rest of my days with my people." Poof!—he vanishes.

"Gee," says the Pole, "it's kind of lonely here. I wish I had my friends back."

✳

What's six miles long and goes four miles per hour?

> A Mexican funeral with only one set of jumper cables.

✳

Why did God give Mexicans noses?

> So they'd have something to pick in the off season.

42

The English teacher in a public school in Spanish Harlem decided it was time for the weekly vocabulary lesson. "What's the difference between select and choose, Ramon?" she asked.

"Select is when you pick something," he answered, "and choose are what Puerto Ricans wear on their feet."

An Irishman, a Frenchman, and a Pole walk into a bar.

The Irishman orders a WW.

"What's a WW?" asks the bartender.

"A whisky and water," he explains.

The Frenchman orders next, and politely requests an RW.

"What's *that?*"

"A red wine," he explains.

The Pole thinks a bit, and finally leans across the bar to ask for a fifteen.

"What the hell is that?" asks the beleaguered bartender.

"A seven and seven," answers the Pole.

Did you hear about the Italian who emigrated to Poland?

He raised the IQ of both countries.

What are the three occasions on which an Italian man visits his priest?

His first communion. When he gets married. Before his electrocution.

43

What do you get when you cross a Puerto Rican and a Chinaman?

A car thief who can't drive.

*

How do you fit forty-seven Puerto Ricans in a Volkswagen?

Use a blender.

How do you get them out?

Doritos.

*

"Did you hear they sent up a Japanese astronaut?"

"No, first I've heard of it."

"Well, I heard them say on the radio that there's a little nip in the air."

*

How do you keep an Englishman happy in his old age?

Tell him a joke when he's young.

*

When the Irishwoman answered her front door it was only to hear the sorry tidings, shouted through the crack of the open door, that her husband had been killed. "And that's not the worst of it, I'm afraid, Ma'am," said the foreman. "He was run over by a steamroller."

"I'm in my bathrobe," said the new widow. "Could you slip him under the door?"

A Pole, an Italian, and a Puerto Rican jump off the Empire State Building. Who lands first?

Answer #1: The Italian, because the Puerto Rican stops to write on the walls, and the Pole stops to ask directions.

Answer #2: Who cares?

Why are there no Puerto Rican doctors?

Because you can't write prescriptions with spray paint.

What does NAACP stand for?

Negroes Are Actually Colored Polacks.

How many people does it take to bury a Puerto Rican?

Five. One to lower the Puerto Rican, and four to lower the radio.

What do you call three Irishmen sitting on the lawn?

Fertilizer.

How many people does it take to bury an Italian?

Two. There're only two handles on a garbage can.

What do you call a Puerto Rican midget?
A speck.

*

What do you get when you cross a Jew and a Puerto Rican?
A superintendent who thinks he owns the building.

*

Two Poles and a black worked for a construction company and got into the habit of working together—until the day the black fell off a scaffold eleven stories high. When the police got to the scene, there wasn't too much left of the fellow, so the officer in charge turned to the two distraught Poles. "Listen, guys," asked the cop, "was there anything distinctive about this man?"

"No, he was just a regular guy," sniffed one of the Poles.

"Hey, wait a minute!" piped up the other. "He had two assholes!"

"Are you bullshitting me?" asked the cop. "How the hell would you know?"

"Because every time we went into the bar around the corner for a beer at the end of the day," said the Pole happily, "the bartender would say, 'Here comes that stupid nigger with the two assholes!'"

What do you get when you cross a Mexican and an octopus?

Got me, but it sure can pick lettuce.

*

A Pole and a Jew were in a bar watching TV when the late-night news came on. The first sensational story was of a berserk woman poised on a window ledge seven stories up.

"I'll bet you a hundred dollars she won't jump," said the Pole to the Jew.

"You got a deal," said the Jew, sticking his hand out a few moments later when the woman plunged to a gory death. The Pole sadly forked over the money and ordered another drink, only to look up in astonishment as the other fellow tugged on his sleeve and tried to hand the hundred dollars back.

"It's all yours," he protested. "You won the bet fair and square."

"Nah," said the Jew, "I saw it all happen on the six o'clock news."

"I saw it happen on the six o'clock news, too," said the Pole, "and I never thought she'd do it *again* at eleven."

*

A Jew, a Pole, and a black man all died on the same day and went to heaven, where they were warmly greeted by St. Peter. "Good to see you guys," said St. Peter. "One quick quiz and I'll be able to formally admit you to heaven."

"Just a sec," said the Jew. "Being a Jew, I've had

47

it rough all my life, and I'd like to know if I can expect any religious persecution in heaven."

"Certainly not," said St. Peter. "Spell *God.*"

"Well, now," said the Pole, "being Polish, I've been treated like shit, and I'd like to make sure I'm not going to encounter any more of that sort of stuff."

"No way," said St. Peter. "Spell *God.*"

"Saint Peter," said the third man, "as you can see, I'm black, and I've had to endure a lot of prejudice in my life. Can I expect any more of that in heaven?"

"Of course not," said St. Peter. "Spell *chrysan-themum.*"

Homosexual

Did you hear about the Polish lesbian?
She likes men.

What do you call a Jewish homosexual?
He-blew.
What do you call an Irish homosexual?
Gay-lick.
What do you call a Chinese homosexual?
Chew-man-chew.
What do you call an Italian homosexual?
A Guinea cocksucker.

A gay riding along in the subway saw a good-looking man sitting opposite him and was instantly smitten. Following him out of the station, he trailed him into an office building and up to an office. What luck! The man was a proctologist, and he signed up for an appointment. But when the examination progressed, the gay's squeals of evident pleasure infuriated the doctor. His job was to cure illnesses, not to titillate, and making that perfectly clear, he tossed the gay guy out.

The gay, however, was really in love and soon telephoned the doctor's office again, claiming a genuine medical problem and insisting on his services. The doctor reluctantly consented to another office visit. Examining the man, he was astonished to find a long green stem, thorns attached, and then another, then another.

"My God," the doctor cried, "you've got a dozen red roses up your ass! Now I warned you, I'm a reputable doctor. Are you up to the same old tricks again?"

"Read the card," gasped the gay, "read the card!"

Two gay guys were talking when one leaned over and said to the other, "You know, I just got circumcised two weeks ago."

"How wonderful," gasped his friend. "You must let me see it."

The first man obliged, pulling down his pants and proudly displaying his cock.

"Ooooh!" shrieked his friend. "You look ten years younger!"

How do you fit four gays at a crowded bar?
    Turn the stool upside down.

What did one lesbian say to another?
 "Your face or mine?"

An obviously gay guy swished onto a bus to face a derogatory sneer from the massive bus driver. "Faggot," he growled, "where're your pearls?"

"Pearls with corduroy!" shrieked the gay. "Are you *mad*?"

How many gays does it take to change a light bulb?
 Seven. One to change the bulb, and six to shriek, "Faaaaabulous!"

What do Polish lesbians use for a lubricant?
 Tartar sauce.

Considering that in order to get married, you have to have a marriage license, what do two lesbians have to get?
 A licker license.

What do you call a gay milkman?
 A Dairy Queen.

Why was the homosexual fired from his job at the sperm bank?

For drinking on the job.

Handicapped

What's the New Jersey state vegetable?
Karen Anne Quinlan.

The mongoloid husband comes home from work and sits down at the kitchen table, hungry for dinner. Soon enough, his mongoloid wife puts down in front of him a plate with a piece of meat on it, nothing else.

"Where're the vegetables?" he asks.

"Oh," replies his wife, "they're not home from school yet."

Bumper sticker: Hire the handicapped—They're fun to watch.

Graffiti:

MUTANTS FOR NUKES

How do you get a one-armed Pole out of a tree?
Wave at him.

The nervous father-to-be was pacing outside the delivery room when finally the doctor emerged. "Oh, doctor!" he cried. "Is it a boy or a girl?"

"I'm afraid I have a bit of bad news," said the doctor gravely. "I'm sorry to have to tell you that your child was not born complete."

The father's face fell, but he said, "Well, I'm sure it can have a happy and complete life in any case."

"That's not all," said the doctor. "I'm afraid your child has no arms or legs."

"Oh," said the father. "At least I understand they're doing wonderful things with braces and prostheses these days."

"It's not going to be easy," said the doctor. "You

54

see, your child was born with no torso. In fact, your child is only a giant ear."

The father sighed and said, "Well, I'm sure my wife and I can make the best of it."

The doctor said, "I'm afraid that's not the worst of it. It's deaf."

What do you get when you cross a mongoloid with a one-legged Pole?

A Polaroid One-Step!

Bob was an avid golfer and, even at seventy-two, could still hit a fine drive. But finally he went in to his doctor to complain that his eyesight was getting so bad that he often couldn't see the ball.

"Well, Bob," said the doctor, "you know, when you get older something's got to go, and there's not much I can do about it. Now, I do have this patient named Joe—he's getting on in years and not as sharp as he used to be and he's deaf as a post, but he's got twenty-twenty eyesight. Why don't you take him with you the next time you go golfing?"

The arrangement seemed a little curious to Bob, but worth a try, and so the next Saturday he found himself out on the fairway with Joe and hit a beautiful drive.

"Well, Joe," he said, turning to the old guy, "did you see it?"

"Oh, yes," said Joe, "clear as day. If only I could remember where it landed."

Who was the meanest man in the world?

> The guy who raped the deaf-and-dumb girl,
> then cut off her fingers so she couldn't yell
> for help.

Little Herbie had been blind since birth. One day at bedtime, his mother told him that the next day was a very special one. If he prayed extra hard, he'd be able to see when he woke up in the next morning.

The next morning she came into Herbie's room to make sure he'd prayed hard the night before. "Well then, open your eyes and you'll know that your prayers have been answered."

Little Herbie opened his eyes, only to cry out, "Mother! Mother! I still can't see!"

"I know, dear," said his mother. "April Fool."

Nine months to the day following their wedding, the Coopers had a baby. Unfortunately, it was born without arms or legs—without even a torso. It was just a head, Still, the Coopers loved and cared for their child, spoiling and indulging it. Finally after twenty years, they took a much-needed vacation, and whom should they meet on the cruise ship but a European doctor who had recently achieved a medical breakthrough. "I know," he said, "how to attach arms and legs to your child, how to make him whole."

The Coopers cut their trip short, rushed home and into the room where the head lay in its crib,

and said, "Honey, Mom and Dad have the most
wonderful surprise for you!"

"No," shrieked the head, "Not another hat!"

Why shouldn't there be any handicapped jokes?
   Because if it weren't for the handicapped,
   we'd never get parking places.

What did the leper say to the prostitute?
   Keep the tip.

What's a leper in the bathtub?
   Stew.

An unfortunate couple had a son who was born
with no legs. What did they name him?
   Neil.

Their daughter was born with one leg. What
did they name her?
   Eileen.

This beautiful young paraplegic was sitting on
the beach in her wheelchair, gazing mournfully
out at the crashing waves, when a handsome guy
came up behind her. "What's wrong?" he asked
gently. "Why do you look so sad?"

"I've never been kissed," she explained, brushing a tear off her cheek.

"Well, I can take care of that," said the fellow, and did, then walked off down the beach feeling pretty pleased with himself.

The next week he was walking down the beach again when what should he see but the same beautiful young paraplegic, looking more down-in-the-mouth than ever. "What's wrong now?" he asked, looking deep into her eyes.

"I've never been fucked," she said sadly.

"No problem," he said, his chest swelling with manly pride. He bent over to lift her from the wheelchair, cradled her gently in his arms, and walked slowly down the pier. Reaching the end, he threw her in the water and shouted, "Now you're fucked!"

Did you hear about the nice woman who gave Ray Charles a ticket to see Marcel Marceau?

The Williams were suitably unhappy when their first child was born with no ears, and their best friends, the Cains, were well aware of this. Preparing for their first visit to see the newborn, Mrs. Cain reminded her husband that at all costs he should avoid any reference to the baby's defect.

In no time at all both couples found themselves cooing over the crib. "Look at those arms," said Mrs. Cain. "He's really going to be able to throw a ball. And those legs—he could be a sprinter. Say, how're his eyes?"

"Terrific," said the proud mother.

"They better be," blurted Cain. "He'll never be able to wear glasses!"

A guy was passing through town on his way across the state when he decided it was time for lunch. He pulled up in front of a little boy sitting on some front steps and asked, "S-s-s-say, k-k-k-kid, d-d-d-you know wh-wh-where I c-c-c-could g-g-get a hot m-m-meal around h-h-here?"

The kid didn't say a word.

"Hey k-k-k-k-kid, d-d-d-don't you know s-s-s-somewhere s-s-s-serving f-f-food around h-h-h-here?"

The kid shook his head, and the tourist drove off in disgust. Just then the boy's mother came out of the house. "Herbie," she said, "you've lived in this town all your life. Don't tell me you don't know somewhere to get a bite of lunch."

"I d-d-d-do," said the kid, "b-b-b-but you th-th-think I w-w-w-wanna get sl-sl-sl-slapped?"

Then there's the sad story of the poor guy who was in a terrible motorcycle accident. When he came out from under the anesthetic, the doctor was leaning over him anxiously. "Son," he said, "I've got some good news and some bad news. The bad news is that you were in a very serious accident, and I'm afraid we had to amputate both your feet just above the ankle."

"Jesus," gasped the patient. "What's the good news?"

"The fellow in the next bed over would like to buy your boots."

What do you say to a one-legged hitchhiker?
"Hop in!"

A blind man and his friend were walking along with the blind man's dog, when the dog simply raised its leg and pissed on the blind man's shoe. To his friend's astonishment, the man reached over and proceeded to stroke the dog's back.

"What the hell are you patting him for?" exclaimed his friend. "The dog just pissed on you!"

"I gotta find out where his head is," said the blind man testily, "so I can kick his ass."

What do you get when a epileptic falls into a lettuce patch?

Seizure salad.

Jokes for the Blind

Religion

What was the Pope's first miracle?
He made a lame man blind.

What was the Pope's second miracle?
He walked under water.

What was the Pope's third miracle?
He cured a ham.

Did you hear about the Pope's plan to redecorate
the Sistine Chapel?
. . . in knotty pine?

You know why the Pope didn't want to accept the
position?
It meant moving into an Italian neighbor-
hood.

What kind of meat does the Pope eat?
Nun.

A rabbi, a priest, and a minister were having a discussion as to how they divided up the collection plate. The minister explained that he drew a circle on the ground, tossed the collection in the air, and that all the money that landed in the circle was for God and all that landed outside was for himself and the parish. The priest said that his system was similar: He just drew a straight line, tossed the money up, and that what landed on one side was for God and on the other for himself and the church. The rabbi admitted that his system worked along somewhat the same lines. "I just toss the plate up in the air," he explained, "and anything God can catch he can keep."

Christ is on the cross, and Peter is down the hill comforting Mary Magdalene when he hears in a faint voice, "Peter . . . Peter . . ."

"I must go and help my Savior," he said and went up the hill, only to be beaten and kicked back down by the Roman centurions guarding the cross. But soon he hears, "Peter . . . Peter" in even fainter tones, and he cannot ignore the call. Peter limps up the hill, leans a ladder against the cross, and is halfway up when the centurions knock over the ladder, beat him brutally, and toss him back down the hill.

Again he hears, "Peter . . . Peter . . ." ever

fainter, and he cannot sit idle. He staggers up the hill, drags himself up the ladder, and finally gets even with Christ's face. Just as the centurions are reaching for the ladder, Christ says, "Peter . . . Peter . . . I can see your house from here."

A little Catholic kid was praying as hard as he could. "God," he prayed, "I really want a car." Jumping up and dashing to the window, he saw that the driveway was empty.

"God," he prayed again, "I really *need* a car." Still no answer to his prayers. Suddenly the kid stood up, ran into his parents' bedroom, and grabbed the statuette of the Virgin Mary off the mantelpiece. He wrapped it up in ten layers of paper, using three rolls of tape and a spool of twine, then stuffed it inside a box at the very bottom of his closet.

"Okay, God," he said, getting down onto his knees again, "if you ever want to see your mother again . . ."

Why does the Pope wear gym shorts?

He doesn't want to look down on the unemployed.

Two nuns were taking a stroll through the park at dusk when two men jumped them, ripped off their habits, and proceeded to rape them.

Sister Gregory, bruised and battered, looked up

at the sky and said softly, "Forgive him, Lord, for he knows not what he does."

Sister Theresa looked over at her and said, "Mine does."

What's black and red and has trouble getting through a revolving door?

A nun with a spear through her head.

Two bishops were discussing the decline in morals in the modern world. "I didn't sleep with my wife before I was married," said one clergyman self-righteously. "Did you?"

"I don't know, said the other. "What was her maiden name?"

Three nuns die and go to heaven, where they are warmly welcomed at the Pearly Gates by St. Peter. "Sisters," he says, "I want to thank you for all your good work on earth. Now there's just a brief formality before I can admit you to heaven: Each of you will have to answer one question." And, turning to the first nun, he asks, "Sister Michael, what is the Mystery of the Trinity?"

"That's the Father, Son, and Holy Ghost," she replies. And the lights flash, the bells go off, and Sister Michael is swept into the Pearly Gates.

Sister Benedicta," asks St. Peter gently, "what is the Mystery of the Virgin Birth?"

"That's the Immaculate Conception," she replied, and she too is swept inside the gates with much flashing of lights and sounding of bells.

Sister Angelica is left alone, shaking a bit with nervousness. St. Peter turns to her and asks, "What, Sister Angelica, were the first words Eve said to Adam?"

Sister Angelica thought it over, beads of sweat starting to appear on her brow, and finally blurted, "Gee, Saint Peter, that's a hard one."

And the bells went off, the gates opened . . .

Jesus was making his usual rounds in heaven when he noticed a wizened, white-haired old man sitting in a corner looking very disconsolate. The next week he was disturbed to come across him again, looking equally miserable, and a week later he stopped to talk to him.

"See here, old fellow," said Jesus kindly, "this is heaven. The sun is shining, you've got all you could want to eat, all the instruments you might want to play—you're supposed to be blissfully happy! What's wrong?"

"Well," said the old man, "you see, I was a carpenter on earth, and lost my only, dearly beloved son at an early age. And here in heaven I was hoping more than anything to find him."

Tears sprang to Jesus' eyes. "Father!" he cried.

The old man jumped to his feet, bursting into tears, and sobbed, "Pinocchio!"

Three Irish women were passing the time of day on the street corner, the street corner that just happened to be opposite the local whorehouse. And when the rabbi went in the door, there was a great clucking of tongues. Next to enter was the Episcopal minister. "Can you believe it?" said one woman to the rest. "The state of the clergy today is positively disgraceful."

Last to enter was Father Flanigan.

"Ah," said the women. "She must be very sick."

A drunk was staggering down the main street of the town. Somehow he managed to make it up the stairs to the cathedral and into the building, where he crashed from pew to pew, finally making his way to a side aisle and into a confessional.

A priest had been observing the man's sorry progress and, figuring the fellow was in need of some assistance, proceeded to enter his side of the confessional. But his attention was rewarded only by a lengthy silence. Finally he asked, "May I help you, my son?"

"I dunno," came the drunk's voice from behind the partition. "You got any paper on your side?"

Three young men presented themselves at the monastery as candidates for entering the monastic order. A stern-looking monk gave them a lecture about the privations of the monastic life, then showed them all into a small room, explaining that there was one preliminary test before they could be accepted as candidates. Ordering them to strip naked, he tied a little bell to each of their penises, then left the room. The next time the door opened, it was to admit a lovely young woman in a bikini, who exited to the tinkling of one of the bells.

"Oh, please, please, give me another trial run," pleaded the guilty party. But the next time the door opened, the lovely young woman was completely naked, and the bell rang even more energetically.

"I'm sorry," explained the monk, "but you are clearly not suited for this life. I must ask you to leave."

Crushed, the young man reached over to pick up his clothes. And the other two bells went off.

∗

Three guys die and are transported to the Pearly Gates, where St. Peter greets them warmly, explaining that there's just one brief formality before they can be admitted to heaven. Each will have to answer one quick question. Turning to the first fellow, he asks, "What, please, is Easter?"

"That's an easy one. That's to celebrate when the Pilgrims landed. You buy a turkey and really stuff yourselves—"

"I'm sorry," interrupts St. Peter. "You're out." Turning to the second man, he asks, "What can you tell me about Easter?"

"No problem," he replies. "To commemorate the birth of Jesus, you go out shopping and get this tree and all these presents—"

"Forget it," says St. Peter, turning in disgust to

the third man. "I don't suppose you'd know anything about Easter?"

"Certainly," he replies. "You see, Christ was crucified and he died, and they took the body down from the cross and wrapped it in a shroud and put it in a cave and rolled this big stone across the entrance—"

"Wait a minute, wait a minute," interrupts St. Peter excitedly, waving for the first two guys to come over. "We got someone here who knows his stuff."

"And after three days they roll the stone away," continues the third guy, "and if he sees his shadow there's going to be six more weeks of winter."

Female Anatomy

A young man was raised in the Australian outback by his father alone, who, not wanting him to get into any trouble, told him to stay away from women. "They have teeth down there," he explained, and let the impressionable boy's imagination do the rest.

In time, however, the fellow's father died. He saw friends getting married and starting families, and he decided it was time to get on with it. So he found himself a willing girl—who was rather disappointed when the consummation consisted of a peck on the cheek alone. The second night she dolled herself up in her sheerest negligée, only to find that once again he pecked her on the cheek, rolled over, and went to sleep. On the third night she caught him before the snores began and proceeded to give him a brief lecture on the birds and the bees and his conjugal duties.

"Oh, no, you don't!" the new husband cried. "I know about you women. You've got teeth down there, and I ain't coming anywhere near."

Well, the bride roared with laughter and invited her husband around the bed for a close inspection. Cautiously he came over and proceeded to look things over with great care. Finally he stuck up his head.

"You're right," he proclaimed. "You've got no teeth, and yours gums are in terrible condition!"

What does an elephant use for a tampon?
A sheep.

Harry came into work on Monday feeling absolutely fine, and so was astonished when his secretary urged him to lie down on the sofa; even more so when his boss took one look at him and ordered him to take the day, if not the week, off. Even his poker buddies wouldn't have anything to do with him, insisting he go straight to bed. Finally, tired of resisting everyone's advice, he went to see his doctor, who took one look at him and rushed over with a stretcher.

"But doctor," he protested, "I *feel* fine."

Well, this was a puzzler, conceded the doctor, who proceeded to refer to the enormous reference tomes behind his desk, muttering to himself. "Looks good, feels good . . . No, you look like hell. Looks good, feels terrible . . . Nah, you feel fine, right?" Thumbing furiously through another volume, he said, "Looks terrible, feels terrible . . . Nope, that won't do it either." Finally, "Looks terrible, feels terrific . . . Aha! You're a vagina!"

Did you hear why Polish women can't use vibrators?

They chip their teeth.

What's the difference between parsley and pussy?

Nobody eats *parsley*.

Did you hear about the new New Wave band called the Toxic Shock Syndrome?

Their new hit's called "Ragtime."

What's green and slimy and smells like Miss Piggy?

Kermit's finger.

It was a hot summer day in the ghetto, and a bunch of little kids were sitting around with no money, nowhere to go, nothing to do. Until someone's dad stuck his head out the window, gave some money to his kid, and told them to get lost and have a good time.

The kid dashed down the block with the others running after him and, much to their astonishment, disappeared into the corner drugstore. After a few minutes he emerged, carrying something in a paper bag. His friends crowded around, demanding to see what he'd bought with the money, and were not at all pleased to see him pull out a box of Tampax.

"Hey, man," they groaned, "we wanted to go out and find ourselves a good time with that money. Why'd you go an' buy *that* shit fo'?"

"Dat's why I *got* it," the boy explained. "It say right here on the box: You can go swimmin', you can go horseback riding . . ."

∗

How can you tell a Pole designed the lower half of a woman's anatomy?

Who else would put the shithole so close to the snack bar?

∗

You know how these days everyone wants a second opinion? Well, this lady had been going to a psychiatrist for years, and one day she decided she'd had enough of it. "Doctor," she said, walking into his office, "I've been seeing you every week for five years now. I don't feel any better; I don't feel any worse—What's the story? I want you to level with me: What's wrong with me?"

"Well," said the doctor, "I'll tell you. "You're crazy."

"Now wait just a minute," the woman protested. "I want a second opinion."

"Okay," said the doctor. "You're ugly, too."

76

On the eve of her wedding the bride-to-be confessed to her best friend that—unbeknownst to her fiancé—she was not a virgin. "No problem," said the friend. "Go out and buy a nice piece of liver and put it up inside you before the time comes. You'll feel nice and tight, and he'll never know the difference."

So the bride went ahead with the plan, and on the wedding night the couple went crazy: They fucked on the floor, on the kitchen table, in the bathroom, in the bed. So the bride was truly astonished to wake up the next morning to find her new husband gone, the only trace of him a note on the bedside table. "Dearest," it read, "I love you very much, but I've realized we can't go on like this and can never have a life together. Farewell. P.S.: Your vagina is in the sink."

Why do tampons have strings?
     So you can floss after you eat.

What's red and has seven little dents in it?
     Snow White's cherry.

This guy walks into a bar and says to the bartender, "I'll have a bourbon and water . . . and get that douche bag down there whatever she'd like to drink," motioning toward a young woman sitting at the other end of the bar.

"Listen, buddy," says the bartender, "this is a

family place, and I'll thank you not to use that sort of language in here."

"Okay, okay," says the guy, "just get me a bourbon and water and get that douche bag a drink too."

"That's a perfectly nice young lady," sputters the bartender, "and—"

"I'm getting thirsty," interrupts the guy, "and you better hurry up with the douche bag's order."

The bartender gives up and moves down the bar, rather shamefacedly asking the woman, "The gentleman at the bar would like to offer you a drink—What'll you have?"

"Vinegar and water, thanks," she replies.

Do you know why women have cunts?
So men will talk to them.

This guy and girl are making out in the back seat of the car, and things are getting pretty hot and heavy. "Put your finger inside me," she asks, and he's only too happy to oblige.

"Put another finger inside me," she orders, moaning in pleasure.

"Put your whole hand inside me."

"Put both hands inside me."

"Now clap."

"I can't!" the guy protests.

"Tight, huh?" she smiles.

How do you fuck a fat girl?
Roll her in flour and go for the wet spot.

Two women are sitting on the front stoop, passing the time. "Damnit," says one to the other, "my husband came home with a dozen roses. I'm gonna have to spend all weekend with my legs in the air."

"Why?" asks her friend. "Don't you have a vase?"

Why do women have two holes?
So that when they're drunk, you can carry them like a six-pack.

What did the blind man say as he passed the fish market?
"Good morning, girls."

What's the difference between garbage and a girl from New Jersey?
Sometimes garbage gets picked up.

How can you tell if your girlfriend's too fat?
If she sits on your face and you can't hear the stereo.

What do Picasso and Princess Anne have in common?

Blue periods.

"Ya got no tits and a tight box," snarled the guy to his girlfriend.

"Get off my back!" she snapped.

Why's pubic hair curly?

You'd poke your eye out if it were straight.

What's the difference between a nymphomaniac and a lover?

A lover stops to eat.

Why do women slap Polish midgets?

Because they're always telling them how nice their hair smells.

Why don't they let women swim in the ocean any more?

They can't get the smell out of the fish.

How can you tell when a Polish woman's not wearing any underwear?

By the dandruff on her shoes.

What do control-top pantyhose and Brooklyn have in common?

Flatbush.

Did you hear about the blind gynecologist?

He could read lips.

"There's a new feminine-hygiene spray out on the market," confided Sandra to Denise at Denise's Tupperware party. "It's called SSY."

"Oh yeah?" said Denise. "How come?"

"That's what you get when you take the PU out of pussy."

What has eighteen legs and two tits?

The Supreme Court.

A doctor was performing a routine gynecological examination when he happened upon a teabag. When he asked his patient about it, she looked up in horror and exclaimed, "Oh my God! Then what could I have put in the hot water?"

There was once a young man who was fixated on the female breast, and he decided to seek professional help. The first test his new psychotherapist performed was one of simple word-association. "Simply say the first word that comes into your mind," the doctor explained. "Orange."

"Breast," said the young man without hesitation.

"Plum," said the doctor.

"Breast," said the young man.

"Grapefruit," said the doctor.

"Breast," said the young man.

"Windshield wipers," said the doctor.

"Breast," said the young man.

"Now just hold on a second," said the doctor. "Oranges I can see reminding you of breasts. Plums, maybe; grapefruit if you're stretching it. But windshield wipers?"

"Sure," said the young man. "First this one, then that one . . ."

There was a promiscuous young couple making out in the back seat of a car. Temperatures were rising and things were getting pretty intense, and finally the girl gasped, "Oh darling, darling, kiss me where it smells."

So he drove her to New Jersey.

What's the difference between a bowling ball and pussy?

You can only fit three fingers in a bowling ball.

Why did God invent booze?

So that fat, ugly girls could have a chance to get laid, too.

Why do little Polish girls put fish in their underwear?

So they'll smell like big Polish girls.

A young couple was making out feverishly on her parents' sofa a few days before their wedding. "Oh baby," moaned the groom-to-be, "please let me see your breasts. I just wanna look." His fiancée blushed and protested, but unbuttoned her shirt.

"Oh honey," he moaned, "let me kiss them."

"Don't you think we should wait till the wedding?" she asked, but it was already too late.

Pretty soon he was begging her to take off her panties. "I just wanna look, I swear," he panted.

"I really think we should wait till the wedding like we said we would," she said, but was finally persuaded by the fact that he was just going to look.

Well, she was adamant about not letting him kiss her down there, insisting that was something special they should wait for. But after a good half hour of artful argument, he had his way. Only to stick his head up a moment later and say anxiously, "Baby, you think that'll *keep* till Sunday?"

Why did God create women?
    Because sheep can't cook.

*

What's a perfect 10?
    A woman about waist-high with no teeth and
    a flat head you can rest your drink on.

*

What's a Cinderella 10?
    A woman who sucks and fucks till midnight
    and then turns into a pizza and a six-pack.

*

Did you hear about the new feminine-hygiene
product?
    It's called Toxic Shock Absorbers.

Male Anatomy

The newlyweds had never slept together and were most eager to consummate their union. The bride in her eagerness insisted on undressing the groom, but stopped dead upon removing his shoes and socks, finding his toes grossly misshapen.

"Not to worry," the groom explained. "A case of toelio when I was a child."

The bride proceeded apace, only to stop again with an expression of shock on her face once she had taken off his pants.

"Nothing but a childhood case of kneesles," he reassured her.

Down to the basics, she reached for his jockey shorts. "I know, I know," she interrupted before her husband could say a word, "nothing but a case of smallcox."

What did the elephant say to the naked man?
    "How d'you breathe through that thing?"

Why did God give black men such huge pricks?
　　Because he was so sorry about what he'd done
　　to their hair.

What's long and hard and full of semen?
　　A submarine.

What did the egg say to the boiling water?
　　"How can you expect me to get hard so fast? I
　　just got laid a minute ago!"

What was the first thing Adam said to Eve?
　　"Stand back! I don't know how big this thing
　　gets!"

What do you get when you cross a rooster with a
peanut-butter sandwich?
　　A cock that sticks to the roof of your mouth.

What do you get when you cross a rooster with an
owl?
　　A cock that stays up all night.

A man came into a bar, sat down at the bar for a drink, and noticed that there was a horse in the back of the room with a big pot of money in front of it. "What's that all about?" he asked the bartender.

"You gotta put a dollar in the pot," explained the bartender, "and you collect the pot if you can make the horse laugh."

The guy went over to the horse, whispered in its ear, and the horse cracked up, fell over, and rolled on the floor in laughter. And the fellow picked up the pot and walked out.

Five years later the same guy walked into the same bar and saw the same horse at the back with another big pot of money in front of it. "It's not so easy," said the bartender. "This time you gotta make the horse *cry*."

The guy walked over to the horse, and in a matter of minutes the horse fell to its knees, sobbing as though its heart were breaking. The guy picked up the pot and was on his way out the door when the bartender stopped him.

"Hey," he said, "at least tell us how you did it."

"Easy," said the guy. "The first time I told him my prick was bigger than his, and the second time I showed him."

✳

The routine practice of circumcision was part of a certain doctor's job, and he found himself reluctant to throw the foreskins away after the operation. So he saved them all up in a jar of formaldehyde. Many years went by, the time came for the doctor to retire from practice, and when cleaning out his office he came across the jar, which by this time contained hundreds of foreskins. It seemed a pity to throw them out after all this time, so, certain that they could be put to some use, he took them down to the tailor around the corner and asked that he make something with them.

"No problem," said the tailor. "Come back in a week."

A week later the tailor proudly presented the doctor with a wallet. "Now wait just a minute!" protested the doctor. "There were literally hundreds of foreskins in that jar, and all I've got to show for it is a measly *wallet*?"

"Relax," said the tailor. "You rub it for a little bit, and it turns into a briefcase."

A black couple took their young son for his first visit to the circus, and by chance their seats were next to the elephant pen. When his father got up to buy some popcorn, the boy piped up, "Mom, what's that long thing on the elephant?"

"That's the elephant's trunk, dear," she replied.

"No, not *that*."

"Oh, that's the elephant's tail."

"No, Mom. Down underneath!"

His mother blushed and said, "Oh, that's nothing." Pretty soon the father returned, and the mother went off to get a soda. As soon as she had left, the boy repeated his question.

"That's the elephant's trunk, son."

"Dad, I *know* what an elephant's trunk is. The thing at the other end."

"Oh, that's the elephant's tail."

"*No.* Down *there.*"

The father took a good look and explained, "That's the elephant's penis."

"Dad, how come when I asked Mom, she said it was nothing?"

The man took a deep breath and replied, "Son, I've *spoiled* that woman."

What's the new Webster's definition of "small?"
"Is it in yet?"

Why does a dog lick his balls?
Because he can.

What do you have when you have two little green balls in your hand?
Kermit's undivided attention.

A Polish couple wants a black baby more than anything in the world, but all their efforts come to nothing. Finally, one day they're walking down the street when they spot a black couple with a beautiful black child in a stroller. So they walk over, explain their greatest desire, and ask the blacks for the secret.

"For one thing," says the black man, "you gotta be eight inches long."

"No problem," says the Pole.

"For another," the black goes on, "you gotta be at least three and a half inches around."

"So *that's* the problem!" exclaims the Pole, turning to his wife. "We've been letting too much light in!"

Did you hear about the masochist who said to her boyfriend, "Give me nine inches and make it hurt."

He fucked her twice and slapped her.

This young man decided that, physically, he simply wasn't adequately endowed. Deciding to take matters into his own hands, he went to a doctor and announced his desire to have his penis surgically enlarged.

The doctor checked things out and told the young man that the only real improvement that could be surgically worked was to implant a section of a baby elephant's trunk.

Rather a radical solution, agreed the patient, but he was adamant. The operation was performed without any complications, and after a few weeks of recuperation the young man decided it was time to try out his new accoutrement.

He asked a lovely young woman of his acquaintance out to dinner at an elegant restaurant. They were having a quiet conversation when his new organ, which had been comfortably resting in his left pants leg, whipped out over the table, grabbed a hard roll, and just as speedily disappeared from sight.

"Wow!" said the girl, truly impressed. "Can you do that again?"

"Sure," said the fellow, "but I don't know if my asshole can stand another hard roll."

Three guys were having an argument about who was more generously endowed. Finally, to settle the matter once and for all, they went up to the top of the Empire State Building and proceeded to unzip their flies.

"Pretty good, huh," said Mort, whose cock was hanging all the way down to the fifty-seventh floor.

"I got you beat cold," said Bill, whose cock was dangling just below a window on the forty-ninth.

They looked over at the third guy, who was dancing a curious sort of jig, jumping from one foot to the other and peering anxiously over the edge of the observation deck.

"What the hell are you doing, Harry?" they asked.

"Dodging traffic," he replied.

*

It was time for sex-education class, and the teacher asked the class, "Children, who can tell me what breasts are?"

"My Mommy has breasts," piped up Rhonda. "She has two of them."

"Right you are, Rhonda," praised the teacher. "Now who can tell me what a penis is?"

"I know," said Eric. "My Daddy has two of them."

"Are you sure?" asked the teacher, puzzled.

"Uh huh," said Eric. "One's about this long," holding his hands about four inches apart, "and looks like mine, and the other's about this long," holding his hands about seven inches apart, "and he uses it to brush Mommy's teeth with."

What's hard and straight going in, and soft and sticky coming out?

Chewing gum.

Two guys were sitting on a bridge passing the time of day and drinking beer, and pretty soon they both had to take a leak. Wanting to impress his companion, the first guy said, "Gee, this water's *cold*."

"And deep," said his friend.

How is a man like a snowstorm?
    Because you don't know when he's coming,
    how many inches you'll get, or how long it'll
    stay.

What's twelve inches long and white?
    Nothing.

Cruelty to Animals

Bumper sticker: NUKE THE WHALES!

A doctor, a lawyer, and an architect were arguing about who had the smartest dog. They decided to settle the issue by getting all the dogs together and seeing whose could perform the most impressive feat.

"Okay, Rover," said the architect, and Rover trotted over to a table and in ten minutes had constructed a full-scale model of Chartres out of toothpicks. Pretty impressive, everyone agreed, and the architect gave Rover a cookie.

"Hit it, Spot," said the doctor, and Spot lost no time in performing an emergency Caesarian section on a cow, with mom and baby coming through the operation in fine shape. Not bad, conceded the other two, and Spot got a cookie from the doctor.

"Go, Fella," ordered the lawyer. So Fella fucked the other two dogs, took their cookies, and went out to lunch.

An elephant was walking along the jungle path when he got a thorn in his foot. He was unable to extract it and gave up all hope until an ant came along the same path. "Ant," said the elephant, "will you get this thorn out of my foot?"

"If I get to do what I want to do," piped the ant.

And what was that, inquired the elephant.

"I want to fuck you in the ass," the ant replied.

Well, the elephant's foot was hurting pretty badly by then, so he told the ant he had a deal (and besides, how bad could it be?). After a few minutes the ant succeeded in working the thorn free. "Are you ready now, elephant?" he piped. Being an honorable elephant, he conceded he was as ready as he was ever going to be and lay still while the ant made his laborious way around to his ass, heaved his tail out of the way, and began to fuck him in the ass.

A monkey high in a tree witnessed the entire transaction. Unable to contain his hysteria at the sight of the ant pumping away at the elephant's rear, he began to heave coconuts down at the beast. He managed to hit the elephant square on the head, eliciting a pained, "Ouch!"

"Take it all, bitch!" squealed the ant.

What can you do with a dog with no legs?
Take it for a drag.

A guy comes into a bar and the first thing he sees in the middle of the room is an enormous alligator. He spins around and is hustling out the door when the bartender says, "Hey, hold it! Come on back in; this alligator's tame. Look, I'll show you."

He comes out from behind the bar, tells the alligator to open its mouth, unzips his pants and whips it out, and stands there with his pecker in the alligator's mouth for a full fifteen minutes.

"Pretty amazing, huh?" he says, turning around and zipping himself up. "You wanna give it a try?"

"Gee, I don't think so," says the first man. "I don't think I could keep my mouth open for fifteen minutes."

An old lady is rocking away the last of her days on her front porch, reflecting on her long life, when all of a sudden a fairy godmother appears in front of her in a beautiful, shining blue gown and tells her she can have any three wishes she wants.

"Well," says the little old lady, "I guess I'd like to be really rich."

And—poof!—her rocking chair turns into solid gold.

"And, gee, I guess I wouldn't mind being changed into a lovely young princess."

And—poof!—she's metamorphosed into a dazzling young woman.

"You get a third wish," reminds the fairy godmother gently, and just then the old lady's cat walks across the porch in front of them.

"Can you change him into a handsome prince?" she asks, and—poof!—there before her stands a young man more handsome than her wildest imaginings.

With a smile that makes her knees weak, he saunters across the porch and whispers in her ear, "Aren't you sorry you had me neutered?"

Did you hear about the Polish fox that caught its paw in a trap?

It gnawed off three feet before it got free.

What does an elephant use for a vibrator?

An epileptic.

What do you do with an elephant with three balls?

Walk him and pitch to the rhino.

A guy comes into a bar with a frog and sets it down next to the prettiest girl there. "This is a very special frog, " he informs her. "His name is Charlie."

"What's so special about this frog?" she asks. He's reluctant to tell her, but when pressed, explains that, "This frog can eat pussy."

The girl slaps him, knocking him off his chair, and accuses him of telling her a filthy lie. But no, he assures her, it's completely true. And after much discussion, she agrees to come back to his apartment to see the frog in action. She positions herself appropriately, the guy carefully takes out the frog, and says, "Okay, Charlie, do your stuff!"

The frog is immobile, despite his owner's exhortations, and the girl starts to snicker.

"Okay, Charlie," says the guy, moving the frog out of the way, "I'm only going to show you one more time."

What's the difference between meat and fish?
    If you beat your fish, it dies.

How do you get virgin wool?
    From ugly sheep.

Why do ducks have webbed feet?
    To stamp out forest fires.
Why do elephants have big, flat feet?
    To stamp out flaming ducks.

What did one Muppet say to the other?
    "I can't talk now—I've got a frog in my throat.

What's red and green and goes up and down and up and down?

A frog in a blender.

What do you get when you cross a Pole and a gorilla?

A retarded gorilla.

A man comes into a tavern and puts his legless dog down on the bar. The bartender comes up to ask him for his order and says, by way of friendly conversation, "What's your dog's name?"

"He doesn't have a name," says the man.

The bartender fixes a second round and, in the process, can't resist asking, "C'mon, what's the dog's name?"

"I told you he doesn't have one."

Over the third round the bartender leans conspiratorially over the bar and says, "I just can't believe you. Every dog has a name."

"Not this one," says the man. "What's the good of it? He can't come when I call."

What do you call a masturbating bull?

Beef Stroganoff.

This blind fellow walked into Macy's with his seeing-eye dog and headed straight for the men's department. Surrounded by pajamas and neckties, he proceeded to come to a stop, pick up his German Shepherd by the hind legs, and swing the dog around and around in a circle.

A startled clerk ran over to him, saying loudly, "Sir . . . may I help you with anything?"

"No thanks," said the blind man, "just looking."

*

What's invisible and smells like rabbit?
    Bunny farts.

*

A flea had oiled up his little flea legs and his little flea arms, had spread out his blanket, and was proceeding to soak up the Miami sun when who should stumble by on the beach but an old flea friend of his.

"Oscar, what happened to you?" asked the flea, because Oscar looked pretty terrible, wrapped up in a blanket, his nose running, his eyes red, and his teeth chattering.

"I got a ride down here in some guy's mustache . . . and he came down by motorcycle. I nearly froze my nuts off," wheezed Oscar.

"Let me give you a tip, old pal," said the first flea, spreading some more suntan oil on his shoulders. "You go to the stewardesses' lounge at the airport, see, and you get up on a toilet seat, and when an Air Florida stew comes in to take a leak, you hop on for a nice, warm ride. Got it?"

So you can imagine the flea's surprise when, a month or so later, while stretched out all warm and comfortable on the beach, whom should he see but Oscar—looking more chilled and miserable than before.

"Listen," said Oscar before the other flea could say a word, "I did everything you said. I made it to the stewardesses' lounge and waited till a really cute one came in, made a perfect landing, and got so warm and cozy that I dozed right off."

"And so?" asked the flea.

"And so the next thing I know I'm on some guy's mustache . . ."

How can you tell when an elephant's got her period?

There's a nickel on the bedstand, and your mattress is missing.

Miscellaneous

How do you fit five comedians in a Volkswagen?

Two in the front seat, two in the back, and Richard Pryor in the ashtray.

What's white and flies across the ocean?

Lord Mountbatten's tennis shoes.

A doctor was walking down the hospital corridor and stopped to speak to the head nurse.

"Oh doctor," she said, "you've got your thermometer stuck behind your ear."

"Shit!" cried the doctor. "Some asshole has my pen!"

Have you ever smelled mothballs?

No! How do you get their legs apart?

Imagine the President's dismay when he woke up one winter morning in the White House to see outside his window, written in pee in the fresh snow, "The President sucks." Furious, he summoned the Secret Service, the police, and the FBI, and told them they had better come up with the culprit—fast.

That afternoon a hapless officer arrived in the Oval Office to give the President the results of their investigation. "We have definitively established that it's the Vice-President's urine," he said, "but I'm afraid it's the First Lady's handwriting."

What's the difference between a rock-and-roller and a pig?

A pig won't stay up all night to fuck a rock-and-roller.

What are the five biggest lies?

"The check is in the mail."

"I won't come in your mouth."

"Some of my best friends are Jewish."

"Black is beautiful."

"I'm from your government, and I'm here to help you."

How many punk rockers does it take to change a light bulb?

Two. One to change the bulb, and the other to kick the chair out from under him.

How many rednecks does it take to eat a 'possum?
  Three. One to eat the 'possum, and two to
  watch for cars.

What's wrinkled and smells like Ginger?
  Fred Astaire's face.

Two cannibals are having dinner together. The guest says to his host, "Your wife sure makes good soup."

"Yeah, but I'm going to miss her," his friend replies.

Harry and Rachel are celebrating their fiftieth wedding anniversary at the Fontainebleau and it's a hell of a party: champagne, caviar, toasts by all of their best friends who've assembled for the occasion. Fianally, tired and happy, the couple retires to their luxurious suite.

"Rachel," says Harry, "you know, this would be the perfect evening if only . . ."

"Oh, Harry," sighs Rachel, "I thought you got over that years ago. You know I don't like it."

"But, Rachel, it's such a special night. Just this once . . ."

"Harry, you know how I feel about this sort of thing."

"I know, I know," pleads Harry, "but you know how much it'll mean to me."

So Rachel finally goes down on him. Just as she's finishing up, the phone rings.

Harry gets up on one elbow and says, "Answer the phone, cocksucker."

Why did the Dairy Queen get pregnant?

Because the Burger King forgot to wrap his whopper.

Why *didn't* the Dairy Queen get pregnant?

Because she went out with Mr. Softee.

Why is the Urban Cowboy's mustache all brown and scuzzy?

He's lookin' for love in all the wrong places.

A guy was sitting having a few at the local pub when he observed a very lovely young woman sitting only a few chairs down. He moved over and proceeded to engage her in general conversation, finally screwing up his courage to ask her out to a movie.

She hauled off and slugged him so hard he landed on his ass on the floor. "Gee," he said, picking himself up, "I guess a blow job is out of the question, huh?"

*

How can you tell the head nurse?

By the dirt on her knees.

What do you call nuts on a wall?
    Walnuts.
What do you call nuts on a chest?
    Chestnuts.
What do you call nuts on a chin?
    A blow job.

*

Why does Dr. Pepper come in a bottle?
    Because his wife died.

*

What did Raggedy Anne say to Pinocchio as she
was sitting on his face?
    "Tell the truth! Tell a lie! Tell the truth! Tell a
    lie!"

*

A man was having a few in the local bar when
he noticed a sailor sitting at the other end of the
bar. The sailor had a completely normal physique
except for one anomaly: his head was tiny, about
the size of an orange.

The man stared at the sailor in puzzlement, and
after a few more drinks screwed up his courage to
go over and ask the sailor how his condition had
come about.

The sailor took the question in good humor,
and explained that some time ago he had been
shipwrecked. "I came to," he explained, "on this
beautiful little beach, and heard this sad little
whimpering sound behind some rocks on the
shore. Investigating, I saw that it was this gor-

geous mermaid who had been stranded on the rocks, so I carried her back to the water's edge. And she was so grateful that she promised to grant me any three wishes. Well, as you can imagine, my first wish was that I get off that god-forsaken island in one piece.

" 'I'll grant you that one after you've had the first two,' she said.

"So next I told her I'd like to be rich beyond dreams. And—whammo—there on the beach appeared a chest full of gold and jewels. And then, being a normal sort of guy—and she was cute, believe me—I asked if we could make love.

" 'Look at me,' said the mermaid. 'It's easy to see I'm not built for that sort of thing.'

"So I says to her, 'Okay, how about a little head!' "

What's the ultimate in courage?
    Two cannibals having oral sex.

For decades two heroic bronze statues, one male and one female, faced each other in a city park, until one day an angel came down from heaven. "You've been such exemplary statues," he announced to them, "that I'm going to give you a special gift. I'm going to bring you both to life for thirty minutes, in which you can do anything you want to." And with a clap of his hand, the angel brought the statues to life.

The two approached each other a bit shyly but soon dashed for the bushes, from which shortly emerged a good deal of giggling, laughter, and shaking of branches. Fifteen minutes later the two statues emerged from the bushes, wide grins on their faces.

"You still have fifteen more minutes," said the angel, winking conspiratorially.

Grinning even more widely, the female statue turned to the male statue and said, "Great! Only this time you hold the pigeon down, and *I'll* shit on its head."

What's the black stuff between an elephant's toes?
Slow natives.

The boss came in and asked the new secretary, "Ellen, do you know the difference between a Caesar Salad and a blow job?"

"No," she replied.

"Great! Let's have lunch."

A woman came to the supermarket, went over to the butcher counter, and announced her desire to buy a Long Island duck. The butcher, a recent employee, obligingly went into the back room and came out with a fine-looking duck.

The woman stuck her finger up the duck's ass and announced, "I'm sorry, this won't do. This is a Maine duck."

The butcher raised his eyebrows, but soon returned with another duck.

"No," pronounced the woman, her finger up the second duck's ass, "this duck is from Minnesota."

Barely restraining himself, the butcher fetched a third duck.

"Now this," said the woman, smiling after performing the same inspection, "this is a Long Island duck. Thank you so much." She was about to leave when she turned back to the counter and asked, "Say, you're new here, aren't you? Where are you from?"

The butcher pulled down his pants, turned around, and said, "You tell me, lady."

An aged couple showed up in their lawyer's office bright and early one morning and announced that they wanted a divorce.

"Gee," said the lawyer, "and at your age and after fifty years of married life. What brought about this decision now?"

"Well you see," explained the couple, "we wanted to wait until the children were dead."

A young guy had gone to his doctor for a routine checkup, and when he came in for the results, the doctor said gravely, "Jerry, I think you'd better sit down. I've got some good news and some bad news."

"Okay, Doc," said Jerry. "Give me the bad news first."

"Well," said the doctor, "you've got cancer. It's spreading at an unbelievably rapid rate, it's totally inoperable, and you've got about three weeks to live."

"Jesus," said Jerry, wiping a bead of sweat off his brow. "What's the *good* news?"

"You know that really cute receptionist out in the front office?"

"You bet!" said Jerry.

"The one with the big tits and the cute little ass?"

"Right!"

"And the long blond hair?"

"Yeah, yeah," said Jerry impatiently.

"Well," said the doctor, leaning forward with a smile, "I'm fucking her!"

Too Tasteless to Be Included in This Book

How do you get a Polish girl pregnant?
Come in her shoe and let the flies do the rest.

What's the difference between a slave and a tire?
A tire doesn't sing when you put the chains on.

What music did they play at Anwar Sadat's funeral?
I Love a Parade.

Two aged child molesters are sitting on a park bench, reminiscing about sexual adventures of their pasts. "Ah," sighs one, "I remember when I had an eight-year-old with the body of a four-year-old . . ."

How many blacks does it take to tar a roof?
A dozen, if you slice 'em thin enough.

An unfortunate fellow was locked up in the state penitentiary doing five to ten for armed robbery. And all he could think of the whole time he was locked up was eating pussy.

The day finally came for his release. He walked out of the prison with the new suit and the ten dollars the officials had given him, and made a beeline for the whorehouse in the nearest town. Slamming down his ten-dollar bill on the front desk, he said, "I wanna eat some pussy!"

"Where've you been," said the greasy fellow behind the desk. "Ten dollars these days don't buy more than a close look."

"Listen, buddy," said the ex-con, pulling him out of his chair by his shirt collar, "I wanna eat some pussy, and I want it *now*."

"Okay, okay," gasped the proprietor, "I'll see what I can do." So the ex-con followed him through to the very back of the whorehouse, through some stained, tattered red curtains, and into a grimy little room where a bedraggled-looking whore lay spreadeagled on a filthy bed. "She's yours for the ten dollars," said the proprietor, and the fellow went at it.

After a little while, he came across a piece of egg. "That's funny," he thought to himself, "I don't think I had eggs for breakfast." But he spat it out and kept eating away. Next he found a piece of chipped beef wedged between his front teeth. "I'm sure I haven't eaten chipped beef this week," he thought, but he kept on. Then he came across the corn.

"I *know* I haven't eaten any corn lately," he said, sitting up. "I think I'm going to be sick."

"Ya know," said the whore, "that's what the last guy said."

Why do blacks smell?
So that blind people can hate them too.

A trucker was carrying a load of bowling balls down the thruway when to his horror, the tailgate unfastened and hundreds of them went rolling across the road. He brought the big truck to a stop as fast as he could and ran back to the scene of the accident—only to see, to his astonishment, dozens of Poles already busy smashing the bowling balls with axes and sledgehammers and any other blunt instruments on hand.

"What the hell are you doing?" he asked.

"You gotta get these nigger eggs before they hatch," they explained.

What's the American dream?
A million blacks swimming back to Africa with a Jew under each arm.

What's the definition of bad acne?
    Waking up in the park with a blind man
    reading your face.

Why does Helen Keller wear skin-tight pants?
    So that people can read her lips.